Earthing

Grounding

"The Power of Earth: A Comprehensive Guide to Earthing and Grounding"

In the hustle and bustle of our modern lives, we often find ourselves disconnected from the natural world around us. Our bodies and minds crave a sense of balance and harmony, yet we spend most of our time indoors, surrounded by electronic devices and insulated from the Earth's natural energy. But

what if there was a simple way to reconnect with nature and revitalize our well-being?

Introducing "Earthing Book: On Grounding," a profound and comprehensive guide that takes you on a transformative

journey to rediscover the healing power of the Earth. Grounding, also known as earthing, is a practice that involves connecting with the Earth's energy by walking barefoot on the ground, lying on the grass, or using specially designed grounding products.

Table Of Contents

"The Power of Earth: A Comprehensive Guide to Earthing and Grounding"

Introduction:

In an increasingly disconnected and fast-paced world, it's **easy** to forget our deep-rooted connection to the Earth. However, the practice of earthing and grounding offers a powerful way to reconnect with nature and harness its healing energy. In this book, we will embark on a journey to explore the concept of earthing and grounding, understand their benefits, and learn practical techniques to incorporate them into our daily lives.

In today's modern society, it is becoming more and more common for people to feel disconnected from the natural world around them. With the rise of technology and the constant busyness of our daily lives, we often forget the profound connection we have with the Earth. However, there is a practice called earthing and grounding that offers us a way to reconnect with nature and tap into its healing energy.

Earthing and grounding are concepts that have been around for centuries, but have recently gained popularity as people seek ways to find balance and harmony in their lives. The idea behind earthing is that by physically connecting with the Earth, such as walking barefoot on the ground or lying on the grass, we can absorb the Earth's energy and restore our own natural energy balance.

Numerous studies have shown the benefits of earthing and grounding on our physical and mental well-being. For example, research has found that spending time outside and connecting with nature can reduce stress levels, improve sleep quality, and even boost the immune system. In addition, grounding has been shown to have a positive impact on inflammation and pain reduction, as well as improving circulation and overall cardiovascular health.

In this book, we will delve into the concept of earthing and grounding and explore how it can benefit our lives. We will learn practical techniques and exercises that can be easily incorporated into our daily routines. For instance, we will discover simple ways to connect with the Earth, such as taking regular walks in nature, practicing yoga or meditation outdoors, or even using grounding mats or sheets while we sleep.

By incorporating these techniques into our daily lives, we can experience a profound shift in our well-being. We may find ourselves feeling more grounded, centered, and connected to the Earth and all its natural beauty. We may notice improvements in our sleep patterns, reduced stress levels, and an overall sense of calm and peace.

Ultimately, earthing and grounding offer us a way to reconnect with the Earth and tap into its powerful healing energy. In a world that often feels disconnected and chaotic, it is important to remember our deep-rooted connection to the natural world. By embracing the practice of earthing and grounding, we can find balance, harmony, and a renewed sense of vitality in our lives. So, let's embark on this journey together, and explore the wonders of earthing and grounding.

Chapter 1: Rediscovering Our Connection with the Earth

- Exploring the historical and cultural roots of earthing and grounding practices.

Earthing and grounding practices have a rich historical and cultural background that dates back centuries. These practices have been rooted in various civilizations and have played a significant role in their belief systems and daily lives. Understanding the historical and cultural roots of earthing and grounding can provide valuable insights into the importance and benefits of these practices.

One of the earliest civilizations to adopt earthing and grounding practices was ancient India. In the ancient Indian system of Ayurveda, which dates back thousands of years, grounding is considered a fundamental principle of health and well-being. The concept of "prithvi" or earth element is central to Ayurveda, and it is believed that connecting with the earth's energy has a balancing effect on the body and mind. Practices such as walking barefoot on the grass or using specific grounding techniques, like placing hands on the ground during meditation, are still widely practiced in India today.

Similarly, Native American cultures have a deep connection to the earth and have incorporated grounding practices into their daily lives for centuries. For many

Native American tribes, the earth is seen as a source of healing and spiritual connection. The practice of walking barefoot on the earth, known as "earthing," is considered a way to absorb the energy of the earth and maintain a harmonious balance with nature. Native American rituals and ceremonies often involve grounding techniques, such as sitting or lying on the ground, to establish a connection with the earth's energy.

In more recent history, the concept of earthing and grounding practices gained attention in the late 20th century with the work of researchers like Dr. James Oschman. Dr. Oschman's research focused on the electrical properties of the human body and the potential benefits of connecting with the earth's electrical energy. He found that the earth's surface is abundant with negatively charged electrons, which can have a positive impact on our health when we come into direct contact with them. This research sparked a growing interest in earthing and grounding practices as a way to combat the detrimental effects of modern lifestyles, such as chronic inflammation and electromagnetic radiation exposure.

Today, the importance of earthing and grounding practices is gaining recognition in the scientific community. Numerous studies have shown that grounding techniques can have a wide range of health benefits, including reducing inflammation, improving sleep quality, and promoting overall well-being. For example, a study published in the Journal of Alternative and Complementary Medicine found that grounding the body to the earth's surface can significantly reduce blood viscosity, which is a key factor in cardiovascular disease.

In conclusion, the historical and cultural roots of earthing and grounding practices span across various civilizations and time periods. From ancient Indian Ayurveda to Native American traditions, the belief in the healing and balancing properties of connecting with the earth's energy has persisted. With the advancements in scientific research, the benefits of earthing and grounding practices are becoming more widely recognized. Incorporating these practices into our daily lives can help us maintain a healthy balance and connection with the earth, leading to improved overall well-being.

- Understanding the scientific basis behind the concept.

To truly understand a concept, it is important to delve into its scientific basis. When it comes to scientific concepts, there is often a wealth of research and evidence that supports their validity. By examining the scientific foundation of a concept, we can gain a deeper understanding of how and why it works.

For example, let's take the concept of gravity. We all know that gravity is the force that keeps us grounded on Earth, but what is the scientific basis behind this concept? Through the work of scientists like Sir Isaac Newton and Albert Einstein, we have come to understand that gravity is the result of the mass of an object bending the fabric of space-time. This bending creates a gravitational pull that attracts other objects towards it. This scientific understanding of gravity not only explains why objects fall towards the Earth, but also how celestial bodies like planets and stars interact with each other.

Another example of the scientific basis behind a concept is the theory of evolution. This concept, first proposed by Charles Darwin, explains how species evolve and adapt over time. The scientific evidence supporting this theory is vast and includes fossil records, genetic studies, and observations of natural selection in action. By understanding the scientific basis of evolution, we can better appreciate the interconnectedness of all living things and how they have evolved to survive and thrive in their environments.

Understanding the scientific basis behind a concept is not only intellectually stimulating, but it also allows us to make informed decisions and judgments. For example, by understanding the scientific basis of climate change, we can recognize the importance of reducing greenhouse gas emissions and taking steps to mitigate its effects. Without this scientific understanding, we may not fully grasp the urgency and magnitude of the problem.

In conclusion, delving into the scientific basis of a concept allows us to gain a deeper understanding of how and why it works. Whether it is the concept of gravity or the theory of evolution, scientific research and evidence provide a solid foundation for these concepts. By understanding the scientific basis, we can make informed decisions and appreciate the interconnectedness of the world around us.

- Unveiling the subtle energy exchanges between humans and the Earth.

Humans are intricately connected to the Earth through subtle energy exchanges that occur on a daily basis. These energy exchanges go beyond the physical realm and encompass the spiritual, emotional, and mental aspects of our being. It is through these exchanges that we are able to tap into the Earth's abundant energy and maintain a sense of balance and well-being.

One way in which we engage in energy exchanges with the Earth is through grounding practices. Grounding involves connecting our energy to the Earth's energy, allowing us to release any excess or negative energy and absorb the Earth's healing and rejuvenating energy. This can be done through activities such as walking barefoot on grass or sand, sitting or lying down on the ground, or even gardening. By engaging in these practices, we are able to recalibrate our energy and restore a sense of calm and stability.

Another form of energy exchange between humans and the Earth is through the use of crystals and gemstones. Crystals are known for their unique vibrational frequencies, which can help align and balance our own energy. For example, rose quartz is often used to promote love and compassion, while amethyst is known for its calming and spiritual properties. By incorporating crystals into our daily lives, whether through wearing them as jewelry or placing them in our living spaces, we can enhance our energy and foster a deeper connection to the Earth.

Additionally, spending time in nature is a powerful way to engage in energy exchanges with the Earth. Studies have shown that spending time in natural environments can reduce stress, improve mood, and increase overall well-being. This is because being in nature allows us to harmonize our energy with the Earth's natural rhythms and vibrations. Whether it's going for a hike in the mountains, taking a swim in the ocean, or simply sitting under a tree in a park, immersing ourselves in nature can help us recharge and replenish our energy.

Furthermore, the food we consume also plays a role in the energy exchanges between humans and the Earth. When we eat fresh, organic, and locally sourced foods, we are not only nourishing our bodies but also aligning ourselves with the Earth's energy. By choosing foods that are grown in harmony with nature and free from harmful chemicals and pesticides, we are ingesting the Earth's vitality and life force. This can have a profound impact on our overall health and well-being.

In conclusion, the subtle energy exchanges between humans and the Earth are vital for maintaining a sense of balance, harmony, and well-being. Through grounding practices, crystal energy, spending time in nature, and consuming nourishing foods, we can tap into the Earth's abundant energy and enhance our own vitality. By recognizing and nurturing this connection, we can lead more fulfilling and balanced lives, both physically and spiritually.

Chapter 2: The Health Benefits of Earthing and Grounding

- Discovering the physical, mental, and emotional benefits of connecting with the Earth's energy.

Connecting with the Earth's energy can have numerous physical, mental, and emotional benefits. One of the most significant physical benefits is the potential for increased energy and vitality. When we walk barefoot on the ground or practice grounding exercises, our bodies absorb the Earth's natural electrical charge. This can help to balance and recharge our own energy systems, leading to improved overall energy levels and a greater sense of vitality.

In addition to the physical benefits, connecting with the Earth can also have a positive impact on our mental well-being. Research has shown that spending time in nature and engaging in activities that connect us to the Earth can reduce stress, anxiety, and depression. This is often attributed to the calming and grounding effect that nature has on our minds. When we immerse ourselves in natural environments, we are able to let go of the constant stimulation and demands of modern life, allowing our minds to relax and recharge.

Furthermore, connecting with the Earth's energy can have a profound effect on our emotional well-being. Many people report feeling a deep sense of peace, joy, and connection when they spend time in nature or engage in grounding practices. This connection to nature can help us to feel more grounded, centered, and in tune with ourselves and the world around us. It can also provide a sense of perspective and remind us of the beauty and abundance that exists in the natural world.

One example of how connecting with the Earth's energy can have a positive impact on our emotional well-being is through the practice of forest bathing. Forest bathing, also known as shinrin-yoku, is a Japanese practice that involves immersing oneself in the sights, sounds, and smells of a forest. This practice has been shown to reduce stress hormones, lower blood pressure, and improve mood and concentration. By simply being present in nature and allowing ourselves to fully experience the sensory stimuli of the forest, we can tap into the healing energy of the Earth and experience a profound sense of peace and well-being.

In conclusion, connecting with the Earth's energy can have numerous physical, mental, and emotional benefits. Whether it's through walking barefoot on the ground, practicing grounding exercises, or immersing ourselves in nature, the Earth offers a powerful source of healing and rejuvenation. By taking the time to connect with the Earth's energy, we can improve our energy levels, reduce stress and anxiety, and experience a greater sense of peace and well-being. So, next time you have the opportunity, take off your shoes, step outside, and let the Earth's energy work its magic.

- Exploring the impact of earthing on inflammation, sleep, stress reduction, and overall well-being.

Earthing, also known as grounding, is the practice of connecting our bodies to the earth's electrical energy. This can be done by walking barefoot on the ground, swimming in natural bodies of water, or using grounding mats or sheets. While earthing may seem like a new-age trend, there is growing scientific evidence to support its positive impact on various aspects of our health and well-being.

One area in which earthing has shown promise is in reducing inflammation in the body. Inflammation is a natural response of the immune system to injury or infection, but chronic inflammation can contribute to a wide range of health issues, including arthritis, heart disease, and even cancer. Studies have shown that earthing can help reduce inflammation by neutralizing free radicals and reducing oxidative stress in the body. One study even found that earthing for just 30 minutes can lead to a significant decrease in markers of inflammation in the blood.

In addition to reducing inflammation, earthing has also been found to improve sleep quality. In today's fast-paced world, many people struggle with sleep problems, which can have a negative impact on their overall well-being. Research has shown that earthing can help regulate sleep patterns by synchronizing our internal body clocks with the natural rhythms of the earth. By improving sleep, earthing can help us wake up feeling more refreshed and energized.

Another benefit of earthing is its ability to reduce stress and promote relaxation. In our modern society, stress has become a common and chronic problem, leading to a wide range of health issues, including anxiety and depression. Earthing has been found to have a calming effect on the nervous system, reducing stress hormones and promoting a sense of calm and well-being. Many people report feeling more relaxed and centered after spending time connecting with the earth.

Overall, the practice of earthing has the potential to greatly improve our overall well-being. By reducing inflammation, improving sleep quality, and reducing stress, earthing can help us feel more balanced and energized. It is a simple and accessible practice that anyone can incorporate into their daily routine. Whether it's taking a walk barefoot on the grass, swimming in the ocean, or using grounding mats, connecting with the earth can have a profound impact on our health and happiness. So next time you have the opportunity, take off your shoes and feel the earth beneath your feet. You may just be surprised at the positive effects it can have on your body and mind.

- Examining scientific studies and anecdotal evidence supporting the health benefits.

Scientific studies and anecdotal evidence both contribute to our understanding of the health benefits associated with certain practices or interventions. By examining these sources of information, we can gain valuable insights into how our choices and behaviors can impact our overall well-being.

Scientific studies are conducted using rigorous methodologies and are designed to provide objective and reliable data. These studies often involve large sample sizes and control groups to ensure the validity of the results. For example, a study published in the Journal of the American Medical Association found that regular exercise can reduce the risk of chronic diseases such as heart disease and diabetes. This study followed a large group of individuals over a span of several years and found a clear correlation between exercise and improved health outcomes.

Anecdotal evidence, on the other hand, is based on personal experiences and observations. While not as scientifically rigorous as controlled studies, anecdotal evidence can still provide valuable insights into the potential health benefits of certain practices. For instance, many people claim that drinking green tea has helped them lose weight and improve their digestion. Although these claims may not be supported by scientific studies, they highlight the positive impact that green tea can have on some individuals.

When examining scientific studies and anecdotal evidence, it's important to consider the limitations of each source.

Scientific studies can be expensive and time-consuming, leading to a scarcity of research in certain areas. Additionally, studies may be funded by organizations with vested interests, potentially biasing the results. On the other hand, anecdotal evidence is subjective and can vary greatly from person to person. What works for one individual may not work for another.

By considering both scientific studies and anecdotal evidence, we can make more informed decisions about our health choices. For example, if a scientific study finds that a certain supplement can improve cognitive function, and numerous anecdotes support this claim, it may be worth considering incorporating the supplement into our routine. However, if scientific studies consistently find no evidence of a health benefit, and anecdotes are inconsistent, it may be wise to approach the practice with caution.

In conclusion, examining scientific studies and anecdotal evidence can provide valuable information about the health benefits associated with certain practices or interventions. While scientific studies offer objective and reliable data, anecdotal evidence provides personal experiences and observations. By considering the strengths and limitations of each source, we can make more informed decisions about our health choices and ultimately improve our well-being.

Chapter 3: Understanding the Science behind Earthing and Grounding

- Diving into the physics and physiology of earthing and grounding.

Earthing and grounding are terms that are often used interchangeably, but they actually refer to different concepts in the world of physics and physiology. Understanding the principles behind earthing and grounding can provide valuable insights into their potential benefits for our overall well-being.

Earthing, also known as grounding, is the practice of connecting our bodies to the Earth's surface by walking barefoot outdoors or using grounding devices indoors. This concept is based on the idea that the Earth has a natural electrical charge and that connecting to it can have positive effects on our health.

Physically, earthing allows electrons to flow from the Earth into our bodies, which can help neutralize free radicals and reduce inflammation. This process is similar to the way antioxidants work in our bodies, but with the added benefit of being directly connected to the Earth's electrical energy.

There have been several studies that have explored the potential benefits of earthing. For example, a study published in the Journal of Alternative and Complementary

Medicine found that earthing can reduce blood viscosity, which is a measure of how thick and sticky our blood is. This can potentially improve circulation and cardiovascular health.

Another study published in the Journal of Environmental and Public Health found that earthing can have a positive impact on sleep quality. Participants who slept on a conductive mattress pad that was connected to a grounding rod reported better sleep and reduced symptoms of insomnia.

In addition to the physical benefits, there are also psychological and emotional benefits to earthing. Spending time in nature and connecting with the Earth can help reduce stress, improve mood, and increase feelings of well-being. This is especially true for people who live in urban environments and may not have as much access to natural spaces.

It's important to note that while there is promising research on the benefits of earthing, more studies are needed to fully understand its effects and mechanisms. However, many people who practice earthing report experiencing positive outcomes, such as improved energy levels, reduced pain and inflammation, and a greater sense of calm and peace.

In conclusion, earthing and grounding are practices that involve connecting our bodies to the Earth's electrical energy. This can have a range of potential benefits for our physical, psychological, and emotional well-being. While more research is needed, many people find value in incorporating earthing into their daily routines, whether it's by walking barefoot on the grass or using grounding devices indoors. So why not give it a try and see if it makes a difference in your life?

- Discussing the role of electrons, electromagnetic fields, and free radicals in the body.

Electrons, electromagnetic fields, and free radicals all play important roles in the functioning of our bodies. Electrons are negatively charged particles that orbit around the nucleus of an atom. They are involved in various chemical reactions and are essential for the transfer of energy within our cells. For example, when we consume food, the electrons in the molecules of that food are transferred to other molecules in our body, allowing us to generate energy.

Electromagnetic fields, on the other hand, are invisible forces that are generated by the movement of charged particles. These fields exist all around us, from the earth's magnetic field to the electromagnetic waves emitted by our electronic devices. In our bodies, electromagnetic fields are involved in many processes, including nerve signal transmission and muscle contractions. For instance, when we move our muscles, electrical signals are sent from our brain to the muscles via electromagnetic fields, allowing us to perform physical activities.

However, while electrons and electromagnetic fields are vital for our well-being, they can also have negative effects when they interact with free radicals. Free radicals are unstable molecules that contain an unpaired electron. They are formed naturally in our bodies as by-products of various metabolic processes. When free radicals come into contact with electrons or electromagnetic fields, they can cause damage to our cells and DNA.

This damage, known as oxidative stress, has been linked to various health problems, including aging, cancer, and cardiovascular diseases. To counteract the harmful effects of free radicals, our bodies have natural defense mechanisms, such as antioxidants. Antioxidants are molecules that can neutralize free radicals and prevent them from causing damage. They can be found in many foods, such as fruits, vegetables, and nuts.

In conclusion, electrons, electromagnetic fields, and free radicals all have important roles in our bodies. Electrons are essential for energy transfer, electromagnetic fields are involved in various bodily processes, and free radicals can cause damage if not properly regulated. To maintain good health, it is important to ensure a balance between these elements. Eating a healthy diet rich in antioxidants can help protect our cells from oxidative stress and minimize the negative effects of free radicals.

- Exploring the mechanisms through which earthing and grounding promote balance and healing.

Earthing and grounding have gained popularity in recent years as natural methods for promoting balance and healing in the body. These practices involve connecting to the Earth's energy by walking barefoot or using grounding devices. While some may consider these practices to be mere pseudoscience, there is scientific evidence to support their potential benefits.

One mechanism through which earthing and grounding promote balance is by reducing inflammation in the body. Inflammation is a natural response to injury or infection, but chronic inflammation can have detrimental effects on our health. Studies have shown that earthing can reduce markers of inflammation, such as C-reactive protein, in the blood. This reduction in inflammation may help alleviate symptoms of conditions such as arthritis, asthma, and autoimmune disorders.

Another way in which earthing and grounding promote balance is by improving sleep quality. In our modern world, many of us are surrounded by electromagnetic fields from electronic devices, which can disrupt our natural circadian rhythm and interfere with sleep. Grounding can help neutralize these electromagnetic fields and restore our body's natural sleep-wake cycle. Research has shown that individuals who practice grounding experience improved sleep duration, decreased sleep latency, and increased sleep efficiency.

Furthermore, earthing and grounding may enhance our overall well-being by reducing stress and promoting relaxation. In today's fast-paced society, stress has become a common and often chronic condition. Grounding has been found to have a calming effect on the nervous system, reducing stress levels and promoting a sense of relaxation and well-being. This practice can help individuals feel more grounded, centered, and connected to the present moment.

To illustrate the potential benefits of earthing and grounding, let's consider an example. Imagine a person who suffers from chronic pain due to arthritis. By incorporating grounding into their daily routine, such as walking barefoot on the grass or using a grounding mat, they may experience a reduction in inflammation and pain. This individual may also find that their sleep improves, allowing them to wake up feeling more refreshed and energized. Additionally, the practice of grounding can help them manage their stress levels, providing a sense of calm and balance in their life.

In conclusion, earthing and grounding offer potential benefits for promoting balance and healing in the body. By reducing inflammation, improving sleep quality, and reducing stress, these practices may enhance our overall well-being. While further research is needed to fully understand the mechanisms behind these effects, many individuals have reported positive experiences with earthing and grounding. So why not reconnect with the Earth's energy and give it a try? You may find yourself feeling more balanced, energized, and at peace.

Chapter 4: Techniques for Earthing and Grounding

- Explaining different methods to connect with the Earth's energy, such as barefoot walking, gardening, and outdoor activities.

Connecting with the Earth's energy is a practice that has gained popularity in recent years as people seek ways to find balance and harmony in their lives. One method of connecting with the Earth's energy is through barefoot walking. By walking barefoot on natural surfaces such as grass, sand, or dirt, individuals can feel a direct connection to the Earth beneath their feet. This practice is believed to help ground and center individuals, allowing them to release any built-up stress or negative energy. It is a simple yet effective way to connect with the Earth's energy and can be easily incorporated into one's daily routine.

Another way to connect with the Earth's energy is through gardening. Tending to a garden not only allows individuals to connect with nature but also provides an opportunity to work with the Earth's energy directly. By planting seeds, nurturing plants, and harvesting the fruits of one's labor, individuals can develop a deeper appreciation for the Earth's cycles and the interconnectedness of all living things. Gardening can also be a meditative practice, allowing individuals to focus their attention on the present moment and cultivate a sense of peace and tranquility.

Engaging in outdoor activities is yet another method to connect with the Earth's energy. Whether it be hiking, camping, or simply spending time in nature, being in the great outdoors allows individuals to immerse themselves in the Earth's natural beauty. Outdoor activities provide a break from the hustle and bustle of daily life and offer a chance to reconnect with one's surroundings. The sights, sounds, and smells of nature can be invigorating and rejuvenating, helping to restore a sense of balance and well-being.

It is important to note that connecting with the Earth's energy is a personal practice, and different methods may resonate with different individuals. Some people may find barefoot walking to be the most effective way to connect, while others may prefer gardening or outdoor activities. The key is to find a method that feels authentic and meaningful to you. By actively engaging with the Earth's energy, individuals can cultivate a deeper connection to themselves, others, and the natural world around them. So whether it be through barefoot walking, gardening, or outdoor activities, take the time to connect with the Earth's energy and experience the benefits it can bring to your life.

- Providing guidance on creating an optimal indoor environment for grounding.

Creating an optimal indoor environment for grounding is crucial for maintaining overall well-being and mental health. Grounding, also known as earthing, is the practice of connecting with the earth's energy to balance and restore our own energy. While spending time outdoors and walking barefoot on natural surfaces like grass or sand is ideal for grounding, it may not always be possible, especially in urban areas or during inclement weather. Therefore, it is important to create an indoor environment that promotes grounding and allows us to reap its benefits.

One key aspect to consider when creating an optimal indoor environment for grounding is the use of natural materials. Natural materials, such as wood, stone, or natural fibers like cotton or wool, have a grounding effect and can help connect us with the earth's energy. Incorporating these materials into our indoor spaces, whether through furniture, flooring, or decor, can enhance the grounding experience. For example, using a wooden desk or a stone meditation altar can provide a sense of connection and stability.

Another important factor to consider is the presence of plants in the indoor environment. Plants not only add beauty and freshness to a space but also have a grounding effect. They absorb toxins from the air, release oxygen, and connect us with the natural world. Having a variety of plants in our indoor spaces, such as potted plants or hanging planters, can create a calming and grounding atmosphere. Additionally, taking care of plants by watering and nurturing them can also be a grounding practice in itself.

Lighting is another element that plays a significant role in creating an optimal indoor environment for grounding. Natural light is the best source of lighting as it mimics the light we receive from the sun. Whenever possible, it is beneficial to have ample natural light in our indoor spaces. This can be achieved by keeping windows unobstructed and using light-colored curtains or blinds that allow sunlight to filter through. If natural light is limited, artificial lighting that closely resembles natural light, such as full-spectrum or daylight bulbs, can be used to create a similar effect.

In addition to these physical elements, creating a quiet and clutter-free space is also essential for grounding. Noise pollution and clutter can disrupt our ability to connect with ourselves and the earth's energy. Therefore, it is important to create a space that is free from excessive noise and distractions. This can be achieved by using soundproofing materials, such as carpets or curtains, and keeping electronic devices or other sources of noise to a minimum. Decluttering the space and keeping it organized can also promote a sense of calm and grounding.

In conclusion, creating an optimal indoor environment for grounding is crucial for maintaining overall well-being. By incorporating natural materials, plants, natural lighting, and creating a quiet and clutter-free space, we can enhance our grounding experience and reap its benefits. Whether it's through the use of a wooden desk, potted plants, or natural lighting, taking steps to create a grounding environment can help us stay connected with the earth's energy, reduce stress, and promote mental and emotional well-being.

- Introducing grounding tools and technologies, including grounding mats and sheets.

Grounding mats and sheets are innovative tools designed to bring the benefits of grounding or earthing into our daily lives. Grounding, also known as earthing, is the practice of connecting our bodies to the Earth's natural electric energy. This connection allows us to absorb the Earth's free electrons, which have been shown to have numerous health benefits.

One popular grounding tool is the grounding mat. These mats are made with conductive materials that enable the transfer of electrons from the Earth to our bodies. They can be placed under a desk or a bed, allowing us to stay grounded even when indoors. By using a grounding mat, we can reduce the build-up of static electricity in our bodies, which can lead to inflammation and other health issues.

Grounding sheets are another effective tool that can be used to promote grounding while we sleep. These sheets are made with conductive fibers that create a direct connection between our bodies and the Earth. By sleeping on a grounding sheet, we can optimize the body's natural healing and regeneration processes. Studies have shown that grounding during sleep can improve sleep quality, reduce pain and inflammation, and enhance overall well-being.

One example of the benefits of grounding tools is their potential to reduce chronic pain. Research has shown that grounding can have a pain-relieving effect by reducing inflammation in the body. By using grounding mats or sheets, individuals with chronic pain conditions, such as arthritis or fibromyalgia, may experience a reduction in their symptoms and an improvement in their quality of life.

In addition to reducing pain, grounding tools have also been shown to improve sleep quality. Many individuals struggle with sleep issues, such as insomnia or restless sleep. By using grounding mats or sheets, we can promote a deeper and more restful sleep. This is due to the calming effect of grounding on the nervous system, which helps to relax the body and mind.

Furthermore, grounding tools can also help to protect our bodies from the harmful effects of electromagnetic fields (EMFs). In today's modern world, we are constantly surrounded by electronic devices that emit EMFs. These EMFs have been linked to various health issues, including increased stress levels and disrupted sleep. By using grounding tools, we can counteract the negative effects of EMFs and create a protective barrier between our bodies and these harmful frequencies.

In conclusion, grounding mats and sheets are valuable tools that can bring numerous health benefits into our daily lives. Whether it's reducing chronic pain, improving sleep quality, or protecting our bodies from EMFs, grounding tools offer a natural and effective solution. By incorporating these tools into our routines, we can promote overall well-being and enhance our connection to the Earth's healing energy.

Chapter 5: Integrating Earthing and Grounding into Daily Life

- Offering practical tips for incorporating earthing and grounding into daily routines.

Incorporating earthing and grounding into daily routines can have numerous benefits for our overall health and well-being. Earthing, also known as grounding, refers to the practice of connecting our bodies to the Earth's natural energy by walking barefoot on grass, sand, or soil, or by using grounding mats or devices. This simple yet powerful practice allows us to absorb the Earth's electrons, which can help reduce inflammation, improve sleep quality, and promote a sense of calm and balance.

One practical tip for incorporating earthing and grounding into our daily routines is to spend some time walking barefoot outside. Whether it's a quick stroll around the backyard or a leisurely walk in a nearby park, taking off our shoes and feeling the Earth beneath our feet can have a profound impact on our well-being. It not only allows us to directly connect with the Earth's energy but also provides an opportunity to reconnect with nature and enjoy the beauty that surrounds us.

Another way to incorporate earthing and grounding into our daily routines is by using grounding mats or devices. These mats are designed to mimic the effects of walking barefoot on the Earth and can be used while sitting, working, or even sleeping. By placing our feet or body on the mat, we can still reap the benefits of earthing, even if we are indoors or unable to go outside. These mats are especially useful for individuals who live in urban areas or have limited access to natural outdoor spaces.

In addition to walking barefoot or using grounding mats, we can also incorporate earthing and grounding into our daily routines by spending time in nature. Whether it's gardening, hiking, or simply sitting under a tree, being in nature provides an excellent opportunity to connect with the Earth's energy and recharge our bodies. Spending time outdoors not only allows us to get our daily dose of earthing but also offers a chance to disconnect from the constant stimulation of technology and reconnect with ourselves and our surroundings.

It's important to note that incorporating earthing and grounding into our daily routines doesn't have to be time-consuming or complicated. Even spending just a few minutes each day engaging in these practices can have a significant impact on our overall well-being. So, whether it's taking a few moments to walk barefoot in the grass, using a grounding mat while working, or spending time in nature, finding ways to connect with the Earth's energy can help us feel more balanced, grounded, and in tune with our bodies.

- Exploring meditation, visualization, and mindfulness practices to enhance the grounding experience.

In today's fast-paced and hectic world, finding ways to stay grounded and centered is essential for maintaining our mental and emotional well-being. One popular approach to achieving this sense of grounding is through the practice of meditation, visualization, and mindfulness. These practices can help us cultivate a deeper connection with ourselves and the present moment, allowing us to navigate life's challenges with greater ease and clarity.

Meditation is a powerful tool for grounding as it encourages us to slow down, quiet the mind, and focus our attention inward. By sitting in stillness and observing our thoughts and sensations without judgment, we can cultivate a greater sense of self-awareness and inner calm. Through regular meditation practice, we can become more attuned to our own needs and emotions, allowing us to respond to life's ups and downs in a more balanced and grounded way.

Visualization is another technique that can enhance the grounding experience. By creating vivid mental images of peaceful and serene environments, we can transport ourselves to a place of calm and tranquility. For example, if we're feeling overwhelmed or anxious, we can close our eyes and imagine ourselves walking along a beautiful beach, feeling the warm sand between our toes and hearing the soothing sound of crashing waves. This visualization can help us relax and shift our focus away from stress and into a more grounded state.

Mindfulness practices, such as mindful breathing or body scan exercises, can also contribute to a greater sense of grounding. By bringing our attention to the present moment and fully experiencing our breath or bodily sensations, we can anchor ourselves in the here and now. This can be particularly helpful during moments of stress or anxiety, as it allows us to detach from racing thoughts and connect with our physical experience. By practicing mindfulness regularly, we can train our minds to be more present and attuned to the present moment, ultimately enhancing our overall sense of grounding.

Incorporating these practices into our daily lives can have profound effects on our mental and emotional well-being. By taking the time to meditate, visualize, and practice mindfulness, we can cultivate a stronger sense of self-awareness, inner calm, and resilience. These practices can help us navigate the challenges of life with greater ease and clarity, allowing us to stay grounded even in the midst of chaos. So, whether it's spending a few minutes each day in meditation, visualizing a peaceful scene, or practicing mindful breathing, exploring these techniques can be a valuable investment in our overall well-being.

- Discussing the importance of nature and outdoor activities for maintaining a strong connection with the Earth.

Maintaining a strong connection with the Earth is essential for our overall well-being and the health of the planet. Nature and outdoor activities play a crucial role in fostering this connection. By immersing ourselves in nature, we can appreciate its beauty, understand its importance, and develop a sense of responsibility towards its preservation.

Spending time in nature allows us to escape the hustle and bustle of everyday life and find solace in the tranquility it offers. Whether it's a hike in the mountains, a walk on the beach, or a picnic in the park, being in nature provides a much-needed break from the constant stimulation of technology and urban environments. The peacefulness we experience in nature can help reduce stress, improve our mental health, and increase our overall sense of well-being.

Additionally, engaging in outdoor activities allows us to develop a deeper understanding of the Earth's ecosystems and the delicate balance they require. For example, when we go camping, we learn to appreciate the importance of leaving no trace and minimizing our impact on the environment. Through activities like gardening or birdwatching, we can witness firsthand the interconnectedness of all living beings and gain a greater appreciation for the intricate web of life.

Outdoor activities also offer an opportunity for physical exercise and connection with our bodies. Whether it's hiking, biking, or playing sports, being active in nature allows us to reap the benefits of exercise while enjoying the beauty of our surroundings. This not only improves our physical health but also strengthens our connection with the Earth as we become more aware of the natural world around us.

Moreover, by engaging in outdoor activities, we become advocates for the protection of our planet. When we witness the destruction caused by pollution, deforestation, or climate change firsthand, we are motivated to take action. By participating in environmental initiatives or supporting organizations that work towards conservation, we can contribute to the preservation of nature and ensure a sustainable future for generations to come.

In conclusion, nature and outdoor activities are essential for maintaining a strong connection with the Earth. By immersing ourselves in nature, we can find peace, improve our mental and physical health, and develop a sense of responsibility towards the environment. Engaging in outdoor activities allows us to appreciate the beauty and interconnectedness of the natural world, while also motivating us to take action to protect it. So, let us prioritize spending time in nature and embracing outdoor activities, not only for our own well-being but also for the health and preservation of our planet.

Chapter 6: Expanding the Benefits: Earthing and Grounding in Different Settings

- Exploring the benefits of earthing and grounding in specific settings, such as homes, workplaces, and healthcare facilities.

Earthing and grounding have been gaining attention in recent years for their potential health benefits. These practices involve connecting the body to the natural electrical charge of the Earth, either by walking barefoot on the ground or using grounding devices. While the scientific research on earthing and grounding is still in its early stages, there are several potential benefits that make them worth exploring.

In homes, earthing and grounding can help reduce the amount of electromagnetic radiation that we are exposed to. With the increasing use of electronic devices and the proliferation of Wi Fi signals, our bodies are constantly bombarded with electromagnetic fields. This can lead to symptoms such as headaches, fatigue, and difficulty sleeping. By grounding ourselves, we can help balance the electrical charge in our bodies and potentially reduce these symptoms.

In workplaces, earthing and grounding can be particularly beneficial for those who work in environments with a high amount of electrical equipment, such as offices or factories. These environments can create a buildup of static electricity in the body, which can cause discomfort and even increase the risk of electrical shock. By grounding ourselves, we can help dissipate this static charge and reduce the risk of injury.

In healthcare facilities, earthing and grounding have the potential to play a role in patient recovery and well-being. Studies have shown that spending time in nature or using grounding devices can help reduce stress, improve sleep quality, and promote overall well-being. This can be particularly important for patients who are confined to a hospital bed or have limited access to natural environments. By incorporating earthing and grounding practices into healthcare settings, we can potentially enhance the healing process and improve patient outcomes.

While the benefits of earthing and grounding are still being studied, there are several practical ways to incorporate these practices into our daily lives. For example, spending time outdoors barefoot, gardening, or using grounding mats or sheets can help us connect with the Earth's electrical charge. It's important to note that earthing and grounding should not replace traditional medical treatments, but rather be used as complementary practices to support overall health and well-being.

In conclusion, exploring the benefits of earthing and grounding in specific settings such as homes, workplaces, and healthcare facilities can provide valuable insights into how these practices can improve our health and well-being. By reducing exposure to electromagnetic radiation, dissipating static electricity, and promoting relaxation and healing, earthing and grounding have the potential to enhance our overall quality of life. While more research is needed, incorporating these practices into our daily routines can be a simple and effective way to support our health and well-being.

- Discussing the potential role of earthing in improving energy efficiency and reducing electromagnetic pollution.

Earthing, also known as grounding, is the process of connecting electrical systems or devices to the Earth's conductive surface. While its primary purpose is to provide safety by preventing electric shocks, there is growing interest in the potential role of earthing in improving energy efficiency and reducing electromagnetic pollution.

One way earthing can improve energy efficiency is by reducing the need for electrical insulation. When electrical systems are properly grounded, they are less likely to experience voltage surges or fluctuations. This means that appliances and devices connected to these systems can operate more efficiently, as they are not constantly adjusting to changes in voltage. This, in turn, can lead to energy savings and lower electricity bills for homeowners and businesses

Additionally, earthing has the potential to reduce electromagnetic pollution. In today's modern world, we are surrounded by electromagnetic fields from various sources such as power lines, electronic devices, and wireless communication systems. These fields can have adverse effects on human health and the environment. By grounding electrical systems, we can help dissipate and redirect these electromagnetic fields, reducing their impact and potentially mitigating their harmful effects.

An example of how earthing can be used to reduce electromagnetic pollution is in the case of stray currents. Stray currents occur when electrical currents find unintended paths to the ground, such as through metal pipes or other conductive materials. These currents can cause corrosion and other damage to infrastructure, as well as contribute to electromagnetic pollution. By properly grounding electrical systems, we can redirect these stray currents and prevent them from causing harm.

Furthermore, the benefits of earthing extend beyond energy efficiency and electromagnetic pollution reduction. Proper earthing can also enhance the performance and lifespan of electrical equipment. By providing a stable reference point, grounding helps to maintain the integrity of electrical systems and protect them from damage caused by voltage spikes or transient surges.

In conclusion, earthing has the potential to play a significant role in improving energy efficiency and reducing electromagnetic pollution. By properly grounding electrical systems, we can enhance the efficiency of appliances and devices, reduce the harmful effects of electromagnetic fields, and extend the lifespan of electrical equipment. As we continue to explore sustainable and environmentally-friendly solutions, earthing should be considered as a valuable tool in our efforts to create a more efficient and less polluting electrical infrastructure.

- Examining the application of grounding in athletic performance and recovery.

Grounding, also known as earthing, is a practice that involves connecting our bodies directly to the Earth's surface. This can be done by walking barefoot on grass, sand, or soil, or by using grounding mats or sheets that are plugged into the ground. While it may sound like a trendy wellness trend, there is actually scientific evidence to suggest that grounding can have a positive impact on athletic performance and recovery.

One of the main benefits of grounding in athletic performance is its potential to reduce inflammation in the body. When we engage in intense exercise, our muscles can become inflamed, leading to soreness and a longer recovery time. However, research has shown that grounding can help to neutralize the positively charged free radicals in our bodies, which are associated with inflammation. By connecting to the Earth's surface, we can absorb negatively charged electrons, which act as antioxidants and help to reduce inflammation.

In addition to reducing inflammation, grounding has also been found to improve sleep quality and reduce muscle soreness. Adequate rest and recovery are crucial for athletes to perform at their best, and grounding can help facilitate this process. By promoting better sleep, grounding allows athletes to wake up feeling refreshed and ready to tackle their training sessions. It also helps to alleviate muscle soreness, allowing athletes to recover more quickly and get back to their training routines sooner.

Furthermore, grounding has the potential to enhance athletic performance by improving balance and stability. When we connect to the Earth's surface, we are grounding ourselves, which can help to stabilize our bodies and improve proprioception. This can be particularly beneficial for sports that require agility and quick movements, such as soccer or basketball. By enhancing balance and stability, grounding can help athletes to move more efficiently and reduce the risk of injuries.

To illustrate the potential benefits of grounding in athletic performance, let's consider the example of a marathon runner. After a long and grueling race, the runner's muscles are likely to be inflamed and sore. By practicing grounding, the runner can reduce inflammation and alleviate muscle soreness, allowing for a quicker recovery. Additionally, grounding can improve sleep quality, ensuring that the runner gets the rest they need to recover properly. With reduced inflammation, improved sleep, and quicker recovery, the runner will be able to resume their training and perform at their best in future races.

In conclusion, grounding has the potential to positively impact athletic performance and recovery. By reducing inflammation, improving sleep quality, reducing muscle soreness, and enhancing balance and stability, grounding can help athletes to optimize their performance and minimize the risk of injuries. Whether it's through walking barefoot on grass or using grounding mats, incorporating grounding into an athlete's routine can be a valuable addition to their training regimen.

Chapter 7: Overcoming Challenges and Misconceptions

- Addressing common misconceptions and concerns surrounding earthing and grounding.

Earthing and grounding are two terms that are often used interchangeably, but they actually refer to different concepts. Earthing, also known as grounding in some regions, is the process of connecting an electrical system to the ground to protect against electrical faults and lightning strikes. Grounding, on the other hand, refers to the process of connecting electrical equipment to the ground to ensure safety and proper functioning.

One common misconception about earthing and grounding is that they are only necessary for large electrical systems or for commercial and industrial buildings. However, this is not the case. Earthing and grounding are important for all electrical systems, regardless of their size or location. Even in a residential setting, earthing and grounding are crucial for protecting against electrical faults and ensuring the safety of the occupants.

Another misconception is that earthing and grounding are only necessary in areas with high levels of lightning activity. While it is true that earthing and grounding can help protect against lightning strikes, they also serve other important purposes. Earthing and grounding help to stabilize electrical systems, reduce the risk of electrical shocks, and protect against electrical fires. Therefore, even in areas with low lightning activity, earthing and grounding are still essential for maintaining a safe and reliable electrical system.

One concern that some people have about earthing and grounding is the potential for electrical interference or "ground loops." Ground loops occur when there are multiple paths for electrical current to flow through the ground, leading to disruptions in the electrical system. However, with proper design and installation, ground loops can be minimized or eliminated. Grounding systems should be designed to ensure a single, low-resistance path for the flow of electrical current, thus reducing the risk of ground loops.

To illustrate the importance of earthing and grounding, consider the example of a home with faulty wiring. Without proper earthing and grounding, an electrical fault could occur, resulting in a live wire coming into contact with a metal appliance or fixture. This could create a dangerous situation, with the potential for electrical shocks or fires. However, with a properly grounded electrical system, any fault would be directed safely into the ground, protecting the occupants and preventing damage to the property.

In conclusion, earthing and grounding are essential for all electrical systems, regardless of their size or location. They protect against electrical faults, stabilize electrical systems, reduce the risk of electrical shocks, and prevent electrical fires. While there may be misconceptions and concerns surrounding earthing and grounding, these can be addressed through proper design and installation. It is important to ensure that all electrical systems, including residential ones, are properly grounded and earthed to ensure the safety and reliability of the system.

- Providing guidance on overcoming obstacles, such as living in urban environments or dealing with physical limitations.

Living in urban environments can present unique obstacles for individuals looking to live a healthy and active lifestyle. The hustle and bustle of city life can make it difficult to find time for exercise or access to outdoor spaces. However, there are ways to overcome these challenges and maintain a healthy lifestyle. For example, individuals can take advantage of the many fitness facilities and classes that are available in urban areas. From gyms to yoga studios, there are a variety of options for individuals to choose from. Additionally, individuals can incorporate physical activity into their daily routines by walking or biking to work, taking the stairs instead of the elevator, or finding nearby parks or green spaces for outdoor activities.

Dealing with physical limitations can also present challenges when it comes to living a healthy and active lifestyle. However, it is important to remember that physical limitations do not have to be a barrier to staying fit. There are many adaptive sports and activities available for individuals with disabilities or physical limitations. For example, wheelchair basketball, adaptive cycling, and swimming are all options for individuals who may have difficulty with traditional forms of exercise. Additionally, there are many resources and organizations that provide support and guidance for individuals with physical limitations, such as adaptive fitness programs or physical therapists who specialize in working with individuals with disabilities.

It is also important to remember that overcoming obstacles is not just about physical activity, but also about finding ways to take care of one's mental and emotional well-being. This can be especially important for individuals living in urban environments, where stress and mental health challenges may be more prevalent. Engaging in activities such as meditation, yoga, or mindfulness exercises can help individuals manage stress and promote overall well-being. Additionally, seeking support from friends, family, or mental health professionals can also be beneficial in navigating the challenges of urban living or dealing with physical limitations.

In conclusion, living in urban environments or dealing with physical limitations can present obstacles to living a healthy and active lifestyle. However, with the right guidance and support, these obstacles can be overcome. By taking advantage of the resources available in urban areas and finding adaptive activities for individuals with physical limitations, it is possible to maintain a healthy lifestyle. Additionally, prioritizing mental and emotional well-being is crucial in navigating these challenges. Overall, with determination and a positive mindset, individuals can overcome these obstacles and live a fulfilling and healthy life.

- Dispelling myths and offering evidence-based explanations to support the practice.

There are numerous myths surrounding various practices and beliefs, and it is crucial to dispel these misconceptions by providing evidence-based explanations. By doing so, we can ensure that accurate information is shared and understood by the target audience.

One common myth is the belief that vaccines cause autism. This misconception gained traction following a now-debunked study that linked vaccines to autism. However, numerous scientific studies have since been conducted, all of which have found no credible evidence to support this claim. In fact, vaccines have been proven to be one of the most effective ways to prevent the spread of infectious diseases and have saved countless lives.

Another widely believed myth is that drinking eight glasses of water a day is necessary for proper hydration. While it is essential to stay hydrated, the specific amount of water needed varies from person to person based on factors such as age, weight, and activity level. The "eight glasses a day" rule is not supported by scientific evidence and is, in fact, arbitrary. Instead, individuals should listen to their bodies and drink water when they are thirsty, ensuring they stay adequately hydrated.

A prevalent myth in the fitness industry is the notion that spot reduction is possible. Many people believe that by targeting specific areas of their body with exercises, they can reduce fat in those areas. However, spot reduction is a myth. When we engage in physical activity, our bodies burn stored fat from all over, not just in one specific area. Therefore, the most effective way to reduce fat is through a combination of regular exercise and a balanced diet.

One myth that has persisted for years is the claim that eating before bed leads to weight gain. While it is true that consuming excessive calories can contribute to weight gain, the timing of when we eat those calories does not significantly affect weight gain or loss. What matters most is the total number of calories consumed throughout the day. As long as we maintain a balanced and calorie-controlled diet, it is unlikely that eating before bed will lead to weight gain.

In conclusion, dispelling myths and providing evidence-based explanations is crucial in ensuring accurate information is shared and understood. By addressing common misconceptions such as the vaccine-autism link, the "eight glasses of water a day" rule, spot reduction in fitness, and eating before bed causing weight gain, we can promote a better understanding of these topics among the target audience. This will empower individuals to make informed decisions based on scientific evidence rather than relying on unsubstantiated beliefs.

In this book, we have delved into the world of earthing and grounding, exploring the science, benefits, and practical techniques to reconnect with the Earth's energy. By incorporating these practices into our lives, we can experience improved well-being, enhanced vitality, and a deeper sense of connection with the world around us. Let us embrace the power of earth and embark on a transformative journey toward holistic health and harmony.